AFFIRMATIONS FOR THE MIND, BODY & SOUL

A Guide for Survivors of Traumatic Events

TWYLIA G. REID

WITH

NASHAREE DAVENPORT

AFFIRMATIONS FOR THE MIND, BODY & SOUL

Copyright © 2018 by *Twylia G. Reid. All rights reserved.*

Biblical verses are taken from the King James Version of The Bible

Published by BROKEN WINGS
Post Office Box 55
Pooler, GA 31322
www.twyliareid.com

All rights reserved. No part of this book may be reproduced, stored in a retrieval system or transmitted in any form or by any means electronic, mechanical, including photocopying, recording, or by any information storage or retrieval system, without permission in writing from the publisher.

Affirmations for the Mind, Body & Soul / 1st Print Edition
Twylia G. Reid

ISBN:978-0-692-07502-9

Printed in the United States of America

FIRST PAPERBACK EDITION

DEDICATION

I dedicate *"Affirmations for the Mind, Body and Soul"* first to my Lord and Savior Jesus Christ for giving me the tenacity and perseverance to write yet another book.

Secondly, to all the survivors of traumatic brain injury and other tragic events, especially my children, **Mylon Flournoy** and **NaSharee Davenport.** Then, to all the members of **Broken Wings Brain Injury Empowerment Group** who have shown me the meaning of true strength through every testimony that's been shared amongst our Broken Wings family. I pray that each of your lives be full of joy and that you will one day discover what God has destined you to do. My message to you is to just keep soaring by the power of God…

I also dedicate this book to anyone affected directly or indirectly by brain injury, traumatic or acquired, as a gift of inspiration, encouragement, and motivation to know that the power of your words can indeed move mountains. So, speak life each and every day and watch the changes occur right before your eyes as we continue to grow as we travel this journey together!

Last, but certainly not least, to anyone affected directly or indirectly by a tragedy of any kind. I understand the emotional and psychological effects that occur after surviving a tragedy have been overlooked far too long. I always say as a survivor that we are our biggest advocate, so I encourage you to speak to those mountains and command them to move!

ACKNOWLEDGEMENTS

When the vision of this book was first given to me, what I had in mind was a workbook type of literary piece. Of course, as I started writing, it became evident that what was demanded was a book to be a guide for survivors to use to build themselves up after experiencing a traumatic event.

I must thank my family for all of their love, support, and prayers as I yet again set out to do what was mandated of me and write material that could be used for God's glory. Thank you, Dexter, for dealing with me through another writing project.

I want to thank Mac Whitfield of iNabi Designs for his amazing God-given talent to tap into this vision and create another cover that speaks life and ministers to your soul. I want to give a wholehearted thank you to Sharlyne Thomas of Sprit of Excellence Writing & Editing Services, LLC, for your keen editing skills and expertise. Your attention to detail is impeccable. I also must thank every single person who purchased a copy of *Broken Wings* and helped catapult me to where I am today. Your prayers, support, text messages, emails, and phone calls mean more to me than any of you will ever know. The love you all have shown me has been immeasurable and I truly thank God for each of you.

Last but certainly not least, to all the newly-found business connections, thank you for pouring into me and encouraging me to keep on keeping on. The knowledge you've shared with me has made me wiser and more capable of being successful on this writing journey, so thank you.

My Message to You...

After writing my first book, *Broken Wings*, so much happened; I don't even know where to begin. The places I've been blessed to go and share my son's and my story of hope and healing have allowed me to meet so many people with countless testimonies.

I have always had a heart for caring for those who have suffered due to any kind of traumatic event. But after our car accident which left my son with a severe traumatic brain injury and years later when my daughter was diagnosed with pseudotumor cerebri, it really made me begin to think about the effects that traumatic events have on survivors or caregivers of the survivor. I know for me, it caused a downward spiral of negatively thinking that my life was over because I knew I'd be a caregiver in one way or another for the rest of my life. Caring for my family and others who've survived traumatic events has led me down several very interesting paths. No matter where I was in my life, I always came across a survivor or caregiver who had experienced the unthinkable but had made it out victoriously. I began to ask God, "Why is this happening?" And although He had a logical reason at the time, I just couldn't understand why.

After years and years of bumping into these survivors and caregivers, I began to mentor and speak positive things into their lives. Why? Because their language was always negative and harsh. They were usually bitter and angry because they just couldn't understand why they were experiencing what they were. I began to share with them the strategy I used to turn my tragedy around to create the life I wanted in spite of the challenges I faced. I educated them on the importance of speaking positive things into their lives daily. I scheduled times throughout the week to meet with them and showed them how to set goals that were geared towards changing the direction of their journey. This sparked a fire in me because the more they implemented these tools, and began to speak positive words and daily affirmations, the better they began to feel over time. They began to go about their daily lives believing that all things were indeed possible if they just believed it and spoke it! I witnessed lives change as chains of bondage were broken. And the best part about it was that it was happening in my life as well because I, too, am a survivor of many traumatic events…my own *private pain.*

God was preparing me to be the solution that so many survivors and caregivers needed! Becoming a caregiver to someone with a severe traumatic brain injury has not been an easy task. Many days and nights of shedding tears and crying out to God have given me a strength that I never knew I possessed. Listening to my own negative speaking was hindering me from seeing the vision God was trying to give me. The negative words my children were speaking due to the challenges and heartache we faced from the devastation we had undergone had finally taken a toll on me! Dealing with the frustrations of not being able to help them find peace during our storms nearly caused me to suffer a nervous breakdown. Until one day, I literally screamed, "ENOUGH!" It was at that moment this vision was birthed; and thus, *Affirmations for the Mind, Body and Soul: A Guide for Survivors of Traumatic Events* was manifested!

Reaching as many survivors and caregivers as I can and being able to give them the will to keep striving and advocating for their loved one, is my calling. Educating them on how to become the strategist of their own destiny will provide them with the tools needed for their journey. Empowering them to go from tragedy to strategy teaching them to create the life they want in spite of health or challenges with the power of positive thinking, will give them the liveliness to persevere. God bless you all.

TABLE OF CONTENTS

INTRODUCTION..13

WHEN THE GOING GETS TOUGH......................16

THE TOUGH GETS GOING..................................18

CHANGE YOUR MINDSET &
YOUR LANGUAGE...21

MORNING AFFIRMATIONS
    I AM..24
    Today I Am and Today I Will............................26
    I Am Filled With Gladness and Joy..................28
    I Am Fully Capable..30
    Today I Am Alive, Alert, and Happy................32
    Today I Will Love and Share Love...................35
    I Am Enough..37
    I Can and I Will..39

AFFIRMATIONS FOR NEW BEGINNINGS
    I Walk but Never Alone...................................42
    I Am a Winner..44
    I Am Open to New Beginnings.........................46
    I Will Forgive Myself..48
    I Embrace Change..50
    Today I Will Make Positive Choices.................52
    I Will Accept Myself...55

GRATITUDE AFFIRMATIONS
I Am Grateful and Thankful for All Things……...58
Today I Am Just Grateful…………….....................60
I Choose Now……………………………………....62
I Am Grateful for New Mercies…………………64
I Am Grateful for Life……………………..............66
Today I Am Grateful for God...…………………68

AFFIRMATIONS WHEN YOU ARE LONELY
I Am Never Alone……………………………….71
I Love and Approve of Myself...…………………73
I Am Important……………………………………76
I Am Enough...………………..………………78

BEDTIME AFFIRMATIONS
I Am Ready for Sleep…………………………….81
I Will Have a Peaceful Sleep……………………..83
I Give Myself Permission……………………….85
I Did My Best Today.…………....………………87

DAILY DOSE
ABC Affirmation………………………...............90
Survivor's Affirmation……………………….…...93
Survivor's Positivity Pledge……………………95

CAREGIVER'S AFFIRMATION……..………....…96

SCRIPTURES THAT SPEAK LIFE
AND KEEP YOU INSPIRED…………….……...99

AFFIRMATIONS MONTHLY
JOURNAL……………………………………...…101

HOW TO USE THIS JOURNAL………..…..……..……103

MONTHLY THEMES..........………..…..…..…………106

PERSONAL GOALS FOR 2018…………..…………..131

NOTE TO SELF...………………………………………132

RECOMMENDED READING...………..….…....……133

ABOUT THE CO-AUTHOR………............……..……..134

ABOUT THE AUHTOR...…..……..…………..………135

INTRODUCTION

Affirmations EMPOWER and INSPIRE You To:

CONTROL…your subconscious instinctive thoughts with uplifting hopeful declarations.

START…focusing on positive change as well as help challenge the negative thoughts when they show up.

ELIMINATE…excuses so your decisions can lead you to your destiny.

CHANGE…your mindset and help you to start seeing abundance instead of limitations.

FEEL…happier, healthier, healed, and set free from all negative experiences that hold you emotionally hostage.

WALK…in the path that God has designed for you—one full of abundant opportunities and joy unspeakable joy.

As you cultivate a habit of practicing these affirmations daily, your overall wellbeing will begin to improve, and your outlook on life will start to change and cause you to feel happy, inspired, motivated, and empowered.

Deciding to make a commitment to have a better life in spite of the challenges that accompany tragedies is critical to you having a positive, productive life. Once the commitment is made, the blinders will fall off, enabling you to see the opportunities that have been before you all along. Yes, that's right: commitment changes you by changing your self-identity and the way you see yourself. Once you begin to see yourself the way God sees you— fearfully and wonderfully made, the head and not the tail, above and not beneath— you've reached the point of no return! Once this shift occurs, your entire world will change.

Traumatic events cause damage and often severe impairment to the psyche that emerges because of a result of a severely challenging or painful event. Many people who have gone through a tragedy of some kind may experience a great deal of stress that can cripple their capability to cope with life. Traumatic events can also leave a person fearful of many things, including obsession and death. Nonetheless, the most damaging effects caused by a traumatic event usually involve the emotional, physical, and cognitive abilities of the survivor or caregiver.

Positive affirmations can be used to transform and convert your life in many astonishing and unusual ways. They can permanently alter the way you think, reprogram your mind to move away from disadvantageous self-beliefs, and allow you to aim for and achieve the life you really want and desire to have.

Your affirmations can literally alter your cataleptic thoughts. They are empowering commands to ensure your distinct development and advancement. Because the power of affirmations lie within the unconscious mind, they influence your thoughts, invite good things into your existence, and provide the successful outcomes you crave and long for.

The words you speak are powerful and full of mysteries only God can reveal. Therefore, when you say these affirmations, say them with confidence in knowing that what you are saying will indeed come to past. Once you begin to speak and believe in the things you are saying, these positive declarations will brighten the very things you seek to attract in life no matter what your current circumstances and conditions may be. When you eliminate mental obstacles, replace the negative self-talk, remove the self-doubt, and develop empowering affirmation habits, you will reap the benefits instantaneously and begin to see a shift in your life!

By saying these affirmations daily and being consistent with your actions, you'll be taking an enormous step towards creating and building the life, future, and legacy you've always wanted.

When The Going Gets Tough

Traumatic events are unique for each person. What you categorize as traumatic others may not and vice versa. For instance, changing jobs can be viewed as a simple everyday task, yet to someone else this change can be highly stressful and distressing. You must be very careful not to judge others when it comes to trauma because each person is unique and possesses diverse stages of understanding.

When I speak of traumatic events, I don't always mean life-threatening circumstances such as fatal accidents, acts of nature, neglect, abuse, or trauma of this kind. While traumatic experiences often are severe and horrifying, they can also be ordinary experiences such as losing a job, daily stress, relocation, and financial or family problems.

Feeling traumatized is often accompanied by the experiences of feeling numb, sad and hopeless, anxious and fearful, confused, angry, irritable, guilty, and the need to be isolated and alone. These feelings become detrimental to your overall well-being causing you to assume the role of a victim.

If you've experienced a traumatic event, and any of the above feelings have attached themselves to you, I want you to begin paying attention to the inclination to start speaking the language of a victim. Although you must face your trauma head on and deal with the devastating challenges that accompany it, you must not overlook that it is very destructive and disempowering to start thinking of yourself as a victim.

When you experience a tragedy, your mind leans toward creating thoughts about how dreadful your life and existence is, and begins to create an identity around suffering and distress. This is known as the victim complex. The moment you begin believing self-pitying thoughts and feelings is the moment you will experience penetrating sorrow. But, when you notice and become conscious of these beliefs, and don't identify with them, you don't suffer and hurt. The more and more you speak positive words your mind, body, and soul will begin to reset, revive, and be restored. Then your transformation will begin.

The Tough Gets Going

Merriam-Webster's definition of the word power is the ability to act or produce an effect. Many may not acknowledge this but, power comes from within. Whatever is going on with you on the outside can never compare to the courage, precision, and kindness that resides within the depths of your soul.

Discovering how to awaken your inner strength, the power within your soul, is all about developing and increasing your self-confidence and self-love. The moment you tap into your self-love, you will realize that nothing can truly stop you from becoming the strategist of your own destiny. How? Because, you will realize that nothing can truly take away the divine inner strength that was placed inside of you by God Almighty Himself! This will in turn empower you to face and conqueror any challenges that come your way.

Just like many of you reading this book, I have gone through many traumatic experiences to include emotional, mental, and even physical abuse. Having survived several abusive relationships, dealing with an emotionally disconnected spouse, going through a self-development process, and now a disabled child had me feeling like I was going insane, among many other things.

Two of the most prevailing and life changing strategies I developed during these hopeless and helpless times were self-love and thought examination. Recognizing that thoughts are NOT facts was a true revelation for me! Learning to take care of myself with loving kindness, realizing that I am who God says I am, and learning that believing thoughts actually generate and produce suffering, grief, and misery delivered me from a lot of anger, resentment, fear, guilt, and shame. But here's the thing: your thoughts don't really mean anything about you unless you believe they do.

When you develop the skill to put some space between you and your reactions it will change your relationship to your thoughts. You will begin to watch them come and go instead of allowing them to resonate and latch on to you.

Positive affirmations help you detach the idea that thoughts are facts. During the course of your day if you begin to experience negative thoughts simply ask yourself are they true, how it makes you feel, and how would things be for you if you didn't hold on to the thought and replaced it with positive ones.

Remember you have the power to command your day. You have the power to change the way you think or feel with your words. Look on the bright side, even when the going gets tough, and find what you can do instead of concentrating on what you cannot do.

Use your words to catapult you into your destiny, and watch how far you soar by the power of God. Hunt the good stuff! If you do you will find it, and lessen the pain of the bad stuff.

CHANGE YOUR MINDSET & YOUR LANGUAGE

Altering your mindset is vital to adapting your new language. Self-expression must now come before safety, and possibilities will now come before protection. This does not mean you should be careless in your decision making, what it means is that now it's time to make decisions that lead to your destiny. Every single one of them!

No matter how much pain or suffering you're going through right now or went through when you experienced your trauma, remember the old saying "this too shall pass". This will help you see the light at the end of the tunnel. Just keep in mind that everything passes, *everything*.

Stay mindful that you are not a victim, but instead a victor. Learning how to access your inner strength to assist in altering your mindset is about training and educating yourself to become aware just how powerful your spoken words really are. Believing what you say about yourself begins deep within. One of the best ways to start identifying with your new language is through a regular regiment of prayer, and meditation practice with positive affirmations.

Most importantly, remember that self-kindness and thought examination are critical strategies for awakening the inherent strength you convey. At first, it may be difficult to believe but with a daily commitment to declare these affirmations you will begin to see and have confidence that you carry strength within you. And, the power of your words can indeed move mountains.

MORNING AFFIRMATIONS

"I AM"

I AM Happy

I AM Healthy

I AM Strong

I AM Prosperous

I AM Protected

I AM Worthy

I AM Confident

I AM Blessed

I AM Thankful

I AM Beautiful/Handsome

I AM Brave

I AM Thrilled About Today

Life's Solution

Today is an incredible day! It will be the best day of your life! Success, prosperity, and abundance in many different forms have naturally found their way into your life today. Gratefully enjoy their manifestations throughout your day and happily share these blessings of abundance with many others to bring happiness to their day as well.

REMINDS ME THAT

_____
_____
_____
_____
_____
_____
_____
_____

"TODAY I AM and TODAY I WILL"

Today I AM grateful for the sunshine on my face.

Today I AM thankful for waking up to see another day.

Today I AM full of unspeakable joy.

Today I AM endowed with peace that surpasses all understanding.

Today I AM given beauty for ashes.

Today I AM unapologetically me.

Today I AM a mountain mover.

Today I AM confident in my abilities.

Today I WILL say yes to God's will.

Today I WILL speak with clarity.

Today I WILL not allow doubt to stop me.

Today I WILL be greater than ever before.

Today WILL be the best day of my life!

Life's Solution

You should not be anxious and worry about anything. God specifically tells you that you should seek Him first and His righteousness, then all the other things you desire will be added to you. This is your assurance that if you put HIM first and seek HIM first, you will not have to worry about the cares of tomorrow. He will take care of those things that you need. Remember, He already knows what they are, so all you need to do is take care of His business and find rest in knowing that in return, He will take care of yours.

REMINDS ME THAT

_____
_____
_____
_____
_____
_____
_____
_____

"I AM FILLED WITH GLADNESS AND JOY"

Today is a day of gladness and joy.

It is a day of peace, love, and happiness.

I am grounded and focused on my tasks for this day.

I am appreciative for my awesome life that is filled with endless possibilities and endless and blessings.

I maneuver through my day with awareness, elegance, and adoration

This will be the best day of my life!

Life's Solution

Everyone wants to be happy. God is the source of all joy and gladness. In Him is where unending satisfaction lies. In Him is where you live, move, and have your being. He possesses great joy, and everyone who accepts Him will enter this true and everlasting joy. He has promised you eternal joy with Him in heaven.

REMINDS ME THAT

_____
_____
_____
_____
_____
_____
_____
_____
_____

"I AM FULLY CAPABLE"

I am fully capable of having an amazing day.

I am strong enough to handle anything that comes my way.

On this day, I believe in myself.

And will turn my dreams into my reality.

I will walk with my head held high.

I will not doubt my ability to succeed.

Today will be the best day of my life!

Life's Solution

Inadequacy is not who you are. Oftentimes desolate feelings overwhelm you and makes you feel less than who you are or what you are cable of doing. Even in the middle of these negative feelings, God calls out to you as His child. No matter how many mistakes you make that takes you away from the plan He has for your life, God never stops loving you. He sees you fully capable and continues to lift you up as His own.

REMINDS ME THAT

_____
_____
_____
_____
_____
_____
_____
_____
_____

"TODAY I AM ALIVE, ALERT, AND HAPPY"

Today as I look at my circumstances, I choose to accept my ability to

take action regarding the choices I make for my life.

I am fearless and will not walk in defeat.

Today as I look at my circumstances, I choose to make my wishes my dreams

and my dreams my reality.

I choose to make them known not only to myself but to the entire world.

On this day, I speak life and I will see the manifestation of it all.

Today as I look at my circumstances, I accept that the selections I make for my forthcoming day will become my divine coach.

Therefore, I choose to listen to and obey the direction that will be given to me

because these directives will move me onward in life as I travel this journey.

Today as I look at my circumstances, I will make healthy choices in my associations and the people I have around me.

Therefore, I choose to feed my mind, body, and soul with only positive thoughts daily.

Today as I look at my circumstances, I choose to show compassion to others who simply do not understand the new me.

Today as I look at my circumstances, I choose to live life anew…

Alive, Alert, and Happy!

Life's Solution

The world is full of things that distract you. Your attention span is shrinking day by day. You must be steadfast, unmovable, always abounding in the word of the Lord. The word of God tells you that your enemies are defeated, but it does not say you are going to defeat your enemies. You live with meaning and purpose and stay alive naturally and spiritually. Being alive, alert, and happy are signs of LIFE. The Bible tells us that we are dead in our sins, but God made us alive with Christ. God sent His Son to die for you so that you may have life and have it more abundantly. So live life in a way that represents Christ…ALIVE, ALERT, and HAPPY!

REMINDS ME THAT

_____
_____
_____
_____
_____
_____
_____

"TODAY I WILL LOVE AND SHARE LOVE"

Today I am willing to share love.

Today I am open to new opportunities.

Today I will allow my inner light to shine bright for the entire world to see.

Today I will allow my talents to encourage and inspire others.

Today I will love myself and those around me unconditionally.

Today I will radiate with joy and glow with confidence.

Today I will be love and only attract love.

Today I will inhale and exhale love.

Today will be the best day of my life!

Life's Solution

Loving others is a command that you have been mandated to do. Renewing your own life starts with renewing your relationship with others. Two of the most important relationships you will ever encounter is the one with God and the one with others. Why? Because loving God and then loving others is a commandment given to the world by God Himself. And if you follow these two commands, you will fulfill every other command that you have been given. YES, today I will love and share God's love!

REMINDS ME THAT

_____
_____
_____
_____
_____
_____
_____
_____

"I AM ENOUGH"

I Am enough and will always be enough.

I Am grateful for my new life and all that I have become.

I Am a forgiving person and will always release those who hurt me.

I Am open to learn new things.

I Am willing to let go of my expectations and allow myself to grow gradually.

I Am now ready to accept a happy and fulfilling life.

Today will be the best day of my life!

Life's Solution

Oftentimes, you base your sense of uniqueness around things you do or what you have or don't have. This can make you unstable in many ways and cause you to feel inadequate. You must remember that you are not your thoughts, feelings, and actions, which change often throughout the course of your life. But your true identity, your God given identity, is one that is unyielding and unshakeable. You must remember that your life doesn't depend on the hopes and dreams you have that may or may not come to pass. But instead, you should learn to trust God and know that He indeed is sufficient and so are you. YES, you are enough!

REMINDS ME THAT

_____
_____
_____
_____
_____
_____
_____

"I CAN AND I WILL"

I CAN have all that I want.

I CAN have all that I need.

I CAN succeed in all that I do.

I CAN achieve all that I set my mind to.

I CAN travel where my dreams take me.

I CAN reach beyond what my eyes can see.

I CAN go where no man has gone before.

And even then, I can go some more.

Why?

Because I CAN, and I WILL!

Life's Solution

The power of your words speaks volumes. The Bible tells us that death and life are in the power of the tongue! Your perception of things matters, so you must be careful of the way you speak about how you perceive those spoken words to be. Saying the words "I Can" brings out the power to refrain your thought process from the undesirable to the desirable.

REMINDS ME THAT

_____
_____
_____
_____
_____
_____
_____
_____
_____
_____
_____

AFFIRMATIONS FOR NEW BEGINNINGS

"I WALK BUT NEVER ALONE"

Today I walk slow, fast, high and low… but never alone.
My head is held high with the confidence of a king, assured that my steps are ordered by God.
For I know that without taking these steps, I can never move forward nor move up in life; so, I must walk and not stand still.

Today I walk slow, fast, high and low… but never alone.
Even if I follow others in the same direction,
my steps are my own.
For when we arrive, we may not be in the same place because I walk with the Spirit; so, my walk is not a race.

Today I walk slow, fast, high and low…but never alone.
Today I will walk by faith, not by sight.
Today I walk but never alone!

Life's Solution

You should always be mindful to spend time with God every day. God's desire is that you walk with Him daily. The Bible says in Psalm 37:23 that "The steps of a good man are ordered by the LORD: and he delighteth in his way." When you walk with God and keep your focus on Him and Him alone, your will is going to always be aligned with His. Keeping your focus on Him will alleviate the distractions that you come across. Walking with God is a journey; it's a lifestyle filled with clarity and tranquility that you can only obtain by walking with Him constantly to receive the nourishment needed to produce healthy fruit.

REMINDS ME THAT

_____
_____
_____
_____
_____
_____
_____
_____

"I AM A WINNER"

I Am willing to start my life anew and try new things.

I Am willing to make mistakes and learn from them each day.

I Am willing to take risks as long as they are safe and will not harm me or others.

I Am the best me there is.

I Am a winner.

I Will see this day through sacred eyes.

I Will shape this day with helpful hands.

I Will end each day with a grateful heart.

Today will be the best day of my life!

Life's Solution

First John 5:4 tells us "For whatsoever is born of God overcometh the world: and this is the victory that overcometh the world, even our faith." The Word also tells you that in a race, all the runners run but only one gets the prize. Whatever you do, do it to the best of your ability; because in the end, your reward comes from God above. Run your race with due diligence. No matter what is happening in your life, keep the attitude that you are indeed a winner. Remember that in all things, we are more than conquerors through Him who loved us and gave Himself for us.

REMINDS ME THAT

_____
_____
_____
_____
_____
_____
_____
_____

"I AM OPEN TO NEW BEGINNINGS"

I am willing to do things I've never done before.

I am willing to explore new and exciting things galore.

I am willing to make mistakes along the way.

"I will not fail as long as I give it my best shot," is all I can say.

I am willing to travel roads of the unknown.

I will continue to learn from the roads traveled from whence I've grown.

I will use my new sets of keys to open new doors

as I unlock new possibilities, being open to new beginnings.

Life's Solution

Letting go of yesterday is the first step to a new beginning. Every fresh beginning comes from some other beginning's end; therefore, you must move forward with great intentions. Although starting over can be challenging, many opportunities to do things differently will present themselves daily. Sir Francis Bacon said, "Seek you first the good things of the mind, and the rest will either be supplied, or its loss will not be felt." As you move forward into your new beginnings, do not trust in your own strength…trust in God. Do not be unprepared; always listen to God. He can talk to you even in the challenging times; so, when you hear His voice, act upon the instructions you are given as you stay open to new beginnings!

REMINDS ME THAT

_____
_____
_____
_____
_____

"I WILL FORGIVE MYSELF"

Today I will forgive myself because
how can I can forgive others if I don't?

Today I will give myself all the love and compassion
I need because
how can I give this to others if I don't?

Today I believe in my own worth because
how can I see the worth of others if I don't?

Today I am willing to be at peace with myself.
I am learning, and I am growing
on this journey; I will keep going.

Today I set my past free,
as free as I can be, and as far as I can see.
You see, today is the day that I truly
believe in ME!

Life's Solution

God does not want you to be mired in guilt and regrets about life. Your past can oftentimes weigh you down. You will never be able to travel back in time to undo any of the things you have done. But you can choose to leave those things behind and move forward. You must remember that forgiving others or yourself is not about condoning the bad things you've done, but it's about realizing that God is waiting on you to turn to Him so that you can move forward. God's opinion of you is all that really matters. So, as you look at yourself today, you are free of your past so ask God for His forgiveness and then forgive yourself. God has granted you mercy and the chance to move forward with a clean slate!

REMINDS ME THAT

_____
_____
_____
_____
_____
_____
_____

"I EMBRACE CHANGE"

Today I will embrace change because
it is the only way I can move forward.

I embrace the end of my old life because
the new one gives birth to new beginnings.

I embrace new beginnings because
they are filled with hope and endless possibilities.

I embrace endless possibilities because
each possibility if filled with endless blessings.

New chances to begin life anew—
Who would want life any other way?
Yes, today I will embrace change!

Life's Solution

Embracing change is the only way to truly grow into a better you. Change is simply a part of life; so, no matter how far you go in life, change will always occur. You often hear that the only thing constant is change, because things around you in your world will forever be changing. Making the decision to change is the key to your success and happiness. Each day, think about your life and ways you are changing and can change. Your attitude toward life and how you choose to live it is always affected by your ability to embrace change. So, stay focused as you embrace change; you will realize that it becomes easier and easier.

REMINDS ME THAT

_____
_____
_____
_____
_____
_____
_____

"TODAY I WILL MAKE POSITIVE CHOICES"

I have the power to choose
who, what, when, where, and how.
I have the power to choose even
if it will be tomorrow or now.

I have the power to choose
one thought over another.
I have the power to choose
if I win or lose.

I have the power to choose
how I move throughout my day.
And today I will change my life
by changing my mind.

Life's Solution

Decisions come in all shapes and sizes and we are all fashioned by them. Each day you get up, you are faced with many different decisions. Some of these decisions are so routine that they have become habits; so, you don't really think about them as much. Making good positive decisions is critical to your wellbeing. Seeking direction from God is always the number one step when it comes to making positive decisions.

When your decisions are in harmony with God's laws and plans, we can stay on track. Making the decision to take action and implement your decisions wisely will lead you to the path of greatness. Remember as Christians, you are chosen by God to receive His amazing grace. Therefore, being chosen, there are duties you must fulfill and choices you must make. So today, chose to make positive choices because they will determine your tomorrow.

REMINDS ME THAT

"I WILL ACCEPT MYSELF"

I WILL accept and value myself.

I WILL forgive and love myself.

I WILL accept my good and my bad.

I WILL be patient with myself when setting my goals.

I WILL not allow fear of how others see me dictate my future.

I WILL not be intimidated by others.

I WILL trust myself.

I WILL express and validate myself.

I WILL use every resource available to me.

I WILL take care of my health, so I can do my best work each day.

I WILL not worry or be full of anxiety.

I WILL not allow pride to stop me from asking for help when needed.

I WILL take one day at a time.

I WILL not give up or quit!

Life's Solution

Oftentimes, you may feel that you are not good enough. Well despite all the things that you think are wrong with you, love yourself anyway. Instead of thinking of yourself as being incomplete, look at yourself each day as being incredible and amazing! Don't go another day without forgiving yourself. Tell yourself each day that you forgive yourself for simply not being perfect. Sometimes it takes simply saying this out loud to yourself and even writing it down to realize that you are indeed good enough. Do something each day to make yourself feel good; this will help you see that you are indeed the source of many wonderful things. Accepting yourself will teach others how to treat you. Whatever it takes…just do it!

REMINDS ME THAT

_____
_____
_____
_____
_____

GRATITUDE AFFIRMATIONS

"I AM GRATEFUL AND THANKFUL FOR ALL THINGS"

I Am thankful for this new day.

I Am filled with love and happiness.

I Am filled with gratitude and thanksgiving.

I Am grateful to see a new day.

I Am grateful for another chance to try and do better than I did yesterday.

I Am grateful for my limbs that work.

I Am grateful for the words that can come out of my mouth.

I Am grateful to be able to breath fresh air, and feel the breeze on my face and the sand underneath my feet.

I Am grateful for who I am and all that I have.

I Am grateful for all the blessings that will be bestowed upon me this day

Today will be the best day of my life!

Life's Solution

You have so much to be grateful for. There are many times when you may get sidetracked and lose focus by life's responsibilities and challenges. This can cause your joy to leave and oftentimes make you bitter and ungrateful. Thankfulness keeps you aware and focused on all the great things God is doing in your life. Remembering to stay humble as you never forget that God is indeed the source of all good things will make it easier for you to be mindful of others. Each day, get up and be thankful no matter what your circumstances are Thank God for all things…especially for His salvation in Jesus Christ! After all, He gave you the greatest gift of all, His son.

REMINDS ME THAT

_____
_____
_____
_____
_____
_____
_____

"TODAY I AM JUST GRATEFUL"

Today I am grateful for life.

Today I am grateful for health.

Today I am grateful for strength.

Today I am grateful for hot summer days.

Today I am grateful for cool autumn days.

Today I am grateful for chilly winter days.

Today I am grateful for food, clothing, and shelter.

Today I am grateful for eyes that can see.

Today I am grateful for ears that can hear.

Today I am grateful for limbs that can move.

Today I am grateful for who I am.

Today I am just grateful!

Life's Solution

Gratitude is a choice, a practice, and an attitude. Steve Maraboli says, "If you want to find happiness, find gratitude." Gratitude helps you to see what is there when you normally see what isn't there. A grateful heart is a magnet for miracles. Fears and doubts disappear when you are grateful. Gratitude causes you to see the good in all things. It can cause you to fall in love with your life, yourself, and your surroundings every single day. Gratitude is the healing factor of all ailments. It's the best medicine for your mind, body, and soul. So, each day you get up, make the decision to just be grateful for everything. It's the best decision you will ever make in life.

REMINDS ME THAT

_____
_____
_____
_____
_____
_____
_____

"I CHOOSE NOW"

I choose to live in the now...
to let go of my painful past as I
allow my present to control my future.

I choose to live in the now...
to grab hold of what I see
as being more than just a possibility.

I choose to live in the now.
My world is a reflection of my mind
with each experience being one of a kind.

I choose to live in the now.
As I seize each moment, I will continue to rise.
I will continue this journey with my eyes on the prize.
I choose to live in the now!

Life's Solution

Whether you realize it or not, you are the result of the decisions that you make each day. It's important for you to be intentional about your choices. Life is full of choices, though some may seem insignificant; however, each one is very important. I'm sure that this morning you had to choose what you were going to wear today. Choosing to sit still and listen, refrain from judging others, or being open to whatever presents itself all play into how your life will pan out. Choose now…choose to smile at others and not care what they think. Choose now…choose to project happiness into your day and the coming weeks and months. Choose now…choose to accept this moment, every single minute of it, because tomorrow is not promised to you. What choices are you going to make NOW that will affect you today and the rest of your life?

REMINDS ME THAT

_____
_____
_____
_____
_____
_____
_____

"I AM GRATEFUL FOR NEW MERCIES"

I am grateful for new mercies each and every day.
God grants them to me; it's the only way.

I am grateful for new mercies each and every day,
and for the love I have inside of me.
God put it there for all to see.

I am grateful for new mercies each and every day,
and for the hope I carry in my heart.
God placed it there to give me a brand new start.

I am grateful for new mercies each and every day,
and for the peace I have in my mind.
God gave me that, too, because I'm one of a kind.

I am grateful for new mercies each and every day.
Each day God grants them to me and sends me on my way.

Life's Solution

Don't forget to thank God and praise Him for His loving kindness and great mercy which is new to you every morning and remains steadfast and sure throughout the day. Yes, God grants you new mercies each and every day. That alone is enough to shout out loud and say, "Thank you!" He loves you just that much. Therefore, you must thank Him for all the ways He has blessed your life, knowing that you are totally undeserving, yet He still loves you. The joy of the Lord is your strength and you can indeed do all things through Him who gives you strength. So, as you go about your day, give God thanks in each and every way. Not only are His mercies new every day, but He is good, and His love endures forever.

REMINDS ME THAT

_____
_____
_____
_____
_____
_____
_____

"I AM GRATEFUL FOR LIFE"

I am grateful for my life for I only get one.

I am grateful for the love that surrounds me each day.

I am grateful for my life and for all that I am.

I am grateful for the grace I am given along the way.

I am grateful for my life and for all that I have.

I am grateful for another chance to live abundantly.

I am grateful for my life and for all that I do.

And most of all, I am grateful that you are here God

to keep me company.

Life's Solution

A grateful heart is a magnet for miracles and blessings. To have peace take precedence of your day and have a vision for your tomorrow, you must learn to express gratitude for life. Gratitude brings a lot of things into your life, including happiness. Being grateful for life shows God that you are indeed happy and grateful for everything He has ever done for you. When you make the decision to be grateful for life, your entire life will turn around and you will not only begin to see the cup half full, you will begin to simply be grateful for just having the cup itself! You have a choice each day you wake up to be grateful for life or not…choose wisely.

REMINDS ME THAT

_____
_____
_____
_____
_____
_____
_____

"TODAY I AM GRATEFUL FOR GOD"

Today I am grateful for God's timing, for HE is an on-time God.
Today I am grateful for God's promises, because they are always YES and AMEN.
Today I am grateful for God's answers, because HE will never lead me astray.
Today I am grateful for God's directions, because HE orders my steps.

Today I am grateful for God's miracles, because HE heals the sick and raises the dead.
Today I am grateful for God's goodness and mercy, because they follow me all the days of my life.
Today and every day I am grateful for God's word, because it is a lamp unto my feet and a light unto my path.
Today I am grateful for God's presence, because HE is with me always even until the end of the world.

Today I Am Grateful for YOU GOD!

Life's Solution

The Bible is filled with commands to give thanks to God. There are many reasons why we should thank Him, such as: "His mercy endureth forever," Psalm 136:3; "for He is good," Psalm 118:29; and "His mercy is everlasting," Psalm 100:5. We've been taught most of our lives that thanksgiving and praise always go together. You cannot effectively praise and worship God without also being thankful. Feeling and conveying appreciation is always good for you. James 1:17 reminds you that God wants you to learn to be thankful for all the gifts He has given you. It is in your best interest to be reminded that everything you have is a gift from Him and Him alone. So, without gratefulness, it is easy for you to fall prey to overconfidence and pride. You begin to believe that you have achieved everything on your own. Thankfulness keeps your hearts in right relationship to your Heavenly Father, the Giver of all good and perfect gifts.

REMINDS ME THAT

_____
_____
_____
_____
_____
_____

AFFIRMATIONS WHEN YOU ARE LONELY

"I AM NEVER ALONE"

I Am never alone;

God is always with me.

He promised to never leave me nor forsake me.

I love and approve of myself.

I feel God's presence and know that He is here with me.

I know that He will never leave me nor forsake me.

I know that He orders my steps daily.

Self-pity is not in my vocabulary.

I know that I Am a winner.

I Am the righteousness of God, and I can do this!

Today will be the best day of my life!

Life's Solution

It is easy to feel alone. Loneliness can be harvested into a giant thanks to your own damaging thoughts and mindset. When you are alone, sad, anxious, or experiencing difficult times, these small thoughts of defeat can take on a big life of their own. It's very important to push past this to stop the giant from growing. This is where you need to step up and be your own hero. In the middle of your fears and irrationality, you awaken to the fact that you are not perfect, BUT you are indeed never alone! God's presence is always there and no matter what you are involved in or where you are, you can rest, knowing that you are winner because He promises to never leave you nor forsake you.

REMINDS ME THAT

_____
_____
_____
_____
_____

"I LOVE AND APPROVE OF MYSELF"

Today I love and approve of myself;
I am all that God says that I am.

Today I love and approve of myself;
I can do all things through Christ who gives me the strength to do so.

Today I love and approve of myself;
I am never alone, and I can do difficult things.

Today I love and approve of myself;
I am beautiful inside and out.

Today I love and approve of myself;
I am worthy of all God has for me.

Today I love and approve of myself;
I know who I am…
a child of the King!

Life's Solution

When it comes to loving yourself, self-approval, and accepting yourself as you are, you may sometimes have a very hard time doing so. In today's world, we usually perform dual roles that carry high expectations. Carrying the title of wife, mom, entrepreneur, daughter, sister, caregiver, or friend can encompass duties and responsibilities that can be overwhelming at times. This can lead to self-doubt, causing you to become your own worst critic. There can be many areas in your life that can cause an imbalance, which oftentimes pushes you into areas of harsh self-criticism.

When this happens, you can lose perspective and make yourself believe that you are worthless and unworthy of all God has for you. You no longer love yourself, and self-sabotage begins to creep in and cause severe damage. This is when you begin to lose your sense of self-worth!

STOP…and go back and read this affirmation again. Stay true to yourself and don't worry about what others are thinking. Approve of yourself today and every day, knowing that you are indeed worthy of all that God has for you!

REMINDS ME THAT

"I AM IMPORTANT"

I am capable, and I am important.

I am worthy, and I am loved.

I am not alone, and I have nothing to prove to anyone.

I am a leader and I am a winner.

I am strong, and I control my destiny.

My words are important and have meaning.

My ideas are one of a kind

I am changing the world.

I am IMPORTANT!

Life's Solution

Many times, we fall into the brokenness of this world and let our weaknesses and uncertainties overtake us. It's easy for you to focus on what others think and say about you instead of living by the truth that is spoken to you from our Lord. You may care more about being accepted by those around you instead of opening up and accepting the love that God has for you. You are important in the eyes of God and He sees you as being fearfully and wonderfully made. God reminds you in Genesis 1:27 that you are created in *His* image. This means that you are created with greatness and created for greatness; and if you keep this in mind, you will be able to find confidence in the hands that created you to be 'enough' each and every day.

REMINDS ME THAT

_____
_____
_____
_____
_____
_____

"I AM ENOUGH"

I am enough and will always be enough.

I am grateful for my new life and all that I have become.

I am a forgiving person and will always release those who hurt me.

I am open to learn new things.

I am willing to let go of my expectations and allow myself to grow gradually.

I love what I see when I look in the mirror.

My imperfections are a part of who I am.

I am now ready to accept a happy and fulfilling life.

Today will be the best day of my life!

Life's Solution

You should never forget that you are a blessed, one of a kind, incredible human being. Each day God graces you with His gift of new mercies. It is up to you to find the blessing in each day to move forward and embrace your healing. You are a part of something bigger than yourself. The journey you are traveling is designed exclusively for you to help you serve your bigger purpose.

You have the choice to change your perspective within your life. You are enough and equipped to handle the challenges you face. You are in control of how you view yourself. Let go of your expectations and allow yourself to grow.

You are healed of anger, sadness, self-doubt, over-thinking, and self-questioning. To have this new beginning you must love and accept yourself and know that you are enough.

REMINDS ME THAT

_____
_____
_____
_____
_____
_____

BEDTIME AFFIRMATIONS

"I AM READY FOR SLEEP"

I am prepared for sleep.

This day has been filled with happiness and peace.

As I prepare to close my eyes, I am grateful for this amazing day.

I separate myself from the activities of this day and let them float away forever.

As I complete this day, I feel calm and safe

I say goodbye to the day's mistakes and misfortunes.

I will keep the nuggets of wisdom and release the rest to the past.

I release the tension of the day as I prepare for tonight's sleep.

I forgive myself and those who may have wronged me.

I am filled with a sense of love, peace, and joy.

I am falling asleep with only good thoughts

I will be revived in the morning and granted with new mercies.

Tomorrow will be the best day of my life…good night!

Life's Solution

Sleep is something that you need to have a healthy life. So, you can rest, knowing that since God never sleeps, He is indeed watching over you. Proverbs 3:24 tells you that when we lie down to sleep, you don't have to be afraid. And when you rest, your sleep will be peaceful. Isn't it amazing, knowing that the peace of God, which transcends all understanding, guards your heart and your mind in Christ Jesus! So, as you sleep, you know that your body will rest securely!

REMINDS ME THAT

_____
_____
_____
_____
_____
_____
_____
_____
_____

"I WILL HAVE A PEACEFUL SLEEP"

Anxiety and fear are released as my mind and body are still

as I prepare for sleep.

I let confident feelings take their place as I feel the darkness

cover my face.

I will have peaceful sleep and enjoyable dreams

as I say goodnight to this day.

When I awake, I will hold on to the newness of the day

and open my heart to all the amazing things that will come

my way.

Tomorrow, my day will be filled with lots of love,

positivity, and hope.

It will be the best day of my life!

Life's Solution

Rest is important to your spiritual walk with the Lord, but many Christians today don't appreciate the value of rest. Rest allows your mind, body, and soul to renew and start with even more strength and focus to handle the challenges of each day. Changing your thinking is an important step to a peaceful night's sleep. There are many reasons why people have difficulty getting to sleep or having a peaceful night's sleep. Most times, worry and fear are the causes of a lack of peace at night. However, God gives you assurance that you can go to bed without fear and anxiety.

REMINDS ME THAT

_____
_____
_____
_____
_____
_____
_____
_____

"I GIVE MYSELF PERMISSION"

I give myself permission to do what is best for me.
I give myself permission to be all that I can be.
I give myself permission to learn all that I want to know.
I give myself permission to grow, and grow, and grow.

I give myself permission to be smart, healthy, and wise.
I give myself permission to keep my eyes on the prize.
I give myself permission to stand up for my own beliefs.
I give myself permission to let go of what I want to release.

Tomorrow I give myself permission to be simply be…just me!

Life's Solution

Most times, we hold ourselves to the highest of standards and hold ourselves more accountable than we do anyone else. Giving yourself permission to move forward is not something that needs to be given to you by others. No matter what occurred today, you have the right to give yourself permission to love yourself and be the best that you can be. No matter what happens, life is going to move forward whether you want it to or not. You don't have to wait on someone to give you permission to try new things in life that can help you advance. Many times, you may find yourself stuck because nobody gave you the green light to proceed and move forward. Remember, this is your life; so, give yourself permission to be all that you can be and make the changes you need to make.

REMINDS ME THAT

_____

_____

_____

_____

_____

"I DID MY BEST TODAY"

I have finished my best on this wonderful day.

I have earned my rest for this quiet evening.

I have performed to the best of my ability.

I have used kindness in all my thoughts and actions.

I have shown affection to everyone in need.

So, I end this day with happiness and joy

as I close my eyes and fall asleep.

Life's Solution

Second Timothy 2:15 tells us, "Study to shew thyself approved unto God, a workman that needeth not to be ashamed, rightly dividing the word of truth." Our God is such an awesome God. He does everything for you, gives you everything you need, heals you when you are sick, comforts you when you are sad, and listens to you when no one else will. So why wouldn't you want to give Him your very best? Your best involves giving God your entire being, so you must do whatever you do with all your heart for the glory of God! Your worship must be from the heart with all admiration and sincerity. You must always give your very best.

REMINDS ME THAT

_____
_____
_____
_____
_____
_____

DAILY DOSE

"ABC AFFIRMATION"

I Am AMAZING and ADORABLE

I Am BRILLIANT and BEAUTIFUL

I Am CARING and CAPABLE

I Am DIVINE and DYNAMIC

I Am EAGER and EFFECTIVE

I Am FUNNY and FORGIVING

I Am GIVING and GRACEFUL

I Am HAPPY and HELPFUL

I Am IMPORTANT and INCREDIBLE

I Am JUBILANT and JOYFUL

I Am KIND and KNOWLEDGEABLE

I Am LOVING and LOYAL

I Am MAGNIFICENT and MOTIVATED

I Am NICE and NEEDED

I Am OUTSTANDING and OVERJOYED

I Am PERSEVERING and PRAYERFUL

I Am QUIET and QUALIFIED

I Am REMARKABLE and RESILIENT

I Am SPECTACULAR and SECURE

I Am THANKFUL and TEACHABLE

I Am UNIQUE and UNSTOPPABLE

I Am VALUABLE and VICTORIOUS

I Am WONDERFUL and WORTHY

I Am XENIAL

I Am YOUNG at heart

I Am ZEALOUS

Life's Solution

Every thought you think and every word you speak creates your future. Affirmations for the mind, body, and soul keep you focused and grounded on the things that are important in life. Positive affirmations can be used to change your thought patterns and transform the way you think and feel about things. They are positive statements to start your day that can help you focus on goals as well as dispose of negative, self-defeating beliefs and program your subconscious mind to help you change your outlook and create the atmosphere you desire in spite of any challenges you face.

REMINDS ME THAT

_____
_____
_____
_____
_____
_____
_____

"Survivor's Affirmation"

I AM a survivor.

I AM able to do all things through Christ who gives me strength.

I AM the best survivor that I can be.

I AM worthy of a fulfilling life.

I AM enough.

I AM able to have a happy life full of joy.

I AM full of tenacity.

I AM courageous and strong.

I AM loveable and teachable.

I AM not what occurred to me.

I AM what I choose to become.

I AM A SURVIVOR!

Life's Solution

The definition of a survivor is a person who deals with a bad situation or affliction and who gets through; or a person who manages to survive through a situation that often causes death. A person who manages well with a family tragedy and remains robust is an example of a survivor. A survivor is a living testimony to show others what it looks like to go through a devastating event and survive. Survivors are resilient and have a history of victory. As a survivor, you have a responsibility to set the world on fire with your truth! There's someone somewhere who needs your light; so go, be, and do the things that you are called to do. Survivors are not victims… we are true champions!

REMINDS ME THAT

_____
_____
_____
_____
_____
_____
_____

"SURVIVORS POSITIVITY PLEDGE"

I WILL NOT LET UNDESIRABLE BELIEFS AND FEELINGS SUCK THE LIFE FROM ME ANY LONGER AND HINDER MY GROWTH.

INSTEAD, I WILL PLACE MY FOCUS ON ALL THE GOOD AND HAPPY THINGS THAT ARE HAPPENING IN MY LIFE.

I WILL THINK IT, FEEL IT, DECREE IT, AND DECLARE IT DAILY.

THIS WILL HELP ME GIVE OUT AND ATTRACT ATMOSPHERES OF POSITIVE ENERGY,

HELPING ME TO BE APPRECIATIVE

FOR ALL THE MAGNIFICENT THINGS

THAT ARE NOW IN MY LIFE… AND THOSE TO COME.

"Caregiver's Affirmation"

I AM grateful for my life just the way it is.

I AM grateful for my family and love them just the way they are.

Today I will create my own sunshine.

I AM whole and powerful, perfect, and strong.

I AM open to learning lessons of growth daily.

I AM not perfect and will not try to be.

I WILL speak life into the person I care for daily.

I WILL stay positive even when I don't feel like it.

I WILL accept the person I care for just as they are.

I WILL think positive each and every day.

I WILL smile even on the bad days.

I WILL do the best I can.

I WILL not try to be all things to all people at any given time.

I WILL not be afraid to say NO when I need to.

I WILL not feel guilty to take care of myself.

I WILL be my own best friend and encourage myself daily.

I WILL be the best caregiver I can be.

I CAN, and I WILL because
I AM A CAREGIVER!

Life's Solution

The life of a caregiver is one of continuous ups and downs. Each day is filled with its own set of challenges that are never alike. It's a life filled with struggles as well as triumphs. Unfortunately, being a caregiver is oftentimes a thankless job that most people never understand. A caregiver's life orbits around this role with little attention paid to his or her own physical health or emotional and mental wellbeing. With so much to attend to, it's easy to understand how negative thoughts, doubts, or frustration creep in. Let each day be the best day of your life by starting with an affirmation.

REMINDS ME THAT

_____
_____
_____
_____
_____
_____

Scriptures That Speak Life and Keep You Inspired

John 3:3 I can see the Kingdom of God because I am born again.

Matthew 6:25-33 I don't worry about everyday life. God knows my needs and meets them because I make His Kingdom my primary concern.

John 14:21 Jesus shows Himself to me because I love Him.

Romans 5:10 Because Jesus died for my sins, I am no longer separated from God. I live in close union with Him.

John 15:8 The fruit I produce brings great joy to God, my Father in Heaven

2 Corinthians 12:9 God's power works best in my weakness.

Colossians 1:29 Through the energy of Christ working powerfully in me, I teach others His truths.

Ephesians 2:9-10 I have been saved, not by works but grace, so that I might do good works. My faith makes me whole in spirit, soul, and body.

Isaiah 40:31 Because I place my hope in the Lord, my strength is renewed.

Luke 24:36 As I follow Jesus, as I walk with Him, I have peace.

John 15:10 Because I obey Jesus, I remain in His love.

1 Corinthians 1:17 The cross of Christ is my power.

Philippians 4:19 My God meets all my needs.

Psalm 46:1 God is my refuge and strength; He is always ready to help me in times of trouble.

Isaiah 40:29 God gives me strength when I am weary and increases my power

Colossians 3:1-2 I set my heart and mind on things above, not earthly things. This gives me peace.

Proverbs 4:23 I guard my heart because it determines the course of my life.

Psalm 62:8 I trust God at all times because He is my refuge.

Affirmations for the Mind, Body & Soul
MONTHLY JOURNAL

This Journal Belongs To

_____

HOW TO USE THIS JOURNAL

This journal is divided into a 12-month plan for use in personal or group study. You will need a Bible. Although I referred to The King James Version here, there are several other translations that may be a tad bit easier to understand. I suggest The Message (MSG) or The New Living Translation (NLT). You will also need a pencil or pen, and a highlighter.

In a group study it's always best to follow along together so everyone will be on the same page when you all meet each week. In individual study, of course there is no need to follow the exact order especially on days immediate concerns need to be prayed about.

As you write your thoughts through this journal remember that you have the power to command your day! The entries that are of a personal nature should be private and for your eyes only. You don't have to share your responses with anyone, not even in a group setting, unless you feel led to do so.

We as individuals are unique in our own way. With this being said, so are our hopes, dreams, and aspirations. The affirmations and positive themes in this journal cover a range of topics, which are to inspire to push you to interpret and apply to your life in any way you like. It's YOUR journal, your life, and your future, so please enjoy the liberty of making it what it needs to be to serve you best.

You will see a theme for each month. You will be prompted to dig deep within yourself and your mind as you explore your inner being. If you feel stuck on any one area, don't worry just move on and come back to it. Remember, this is YOUR journal, YOUR life, and YOUR future.

The most important thing is just START JOURNALING! Explore your thoughts, identify those that are unhealthy and unhelpful and begin the process of turning them around by focusing on the positive instead of the negative.

Determine what thoughts need to be let go and which thoughts need to stay. Letting go of the negatives to embrace the positives begins now. Each day before you start journaling, visualize what you want to be, what you want to have, and where you want to go in life, and make the choice to change your attitude and improve your life.

You possess the courage and the strength to be, know, and do all you can to have the life you want in spite of the challenges you face.

I wish you lots of love, joy, peace that surpasses all understanding, and abundance in all areas of your life from this day forward.

-Twylia

MONTHLY THEMES

JANUARY............................New Year, New Me
FEBRUARY….…..…...….………Love Is in the Air
MARCH....….…........….…………….…..Make a Wish
APRIL…..…….…....…New Beginnings and Fresh Starts
MAY......…………….….……Honor and Appreciation
JUNE…….......………………..…………Fun in the Sun
JULY…………....…………..Traditions and Freedom
AUGUST……...…...….……..Old Habits Die Hard
SEPTEMBER...….A New Season (Character Building)
OCTOBER……...………..………Knowledge is Power
NOVEMBER…………..Gratitude Changes Attitudes
DECEMBER……..……...……………….Reflections

JANUARY

> *Affirmation: I will be the best me I can be this year.*

Many times, we say with a New Year comes a New Me. What changes can you make to better yourself?

FEBRUARY

Affirmation: I am worthy of love and allow myself to show love to others.

There are many ways you can show LOVE. When love is shown the world smiles. How do you show someone that you love them?

_____

_____

_____

_____

_____

_____

_____

_____

_____

MARCH

Affirmation: I am constantly striving to be all I can be each and every day.

Four Leaf Clovers are believed to bring good luck your way. What do you find yourself wishing for in life that you could do over again?

_____
_____
_____
_____
_____
_____
_____
_____
_____
_____
_____

APRIL

Affirmation: I am willing to believe that I can do all things through Christ who gives me the strength.

With spring brings a fresh start and new beginnings. New life starts while flowers are blooming. What's something that symbolizes a fresh start to you?

_____

_____

_____

_____

_____

_____

_____

_____

MAY

> *Affirmation: I am willing to honor the people in my life who encourage and inspire me.*

Many sacrificed and served to make sure we can enjoy the freedoms of life. What are some ways you can honor someone who's played a significant role in your life?

_____
_____
_____
_____
_____
_____
_____
_____
_____

JUNE

Affirmation: I will live my life to the fullest potential each day.

Fun in the sun can be refreshing and revitalizing. Summer brings joy, happiness, and reunions. What are some ways you enjoy yourself on a sunny day?

_____
_____
_____
_____
_____
_____
_____
_____
_____
_____
_____
_____

JULY

> *Affirmation: I am making positive changes and influences on the world and people in my life.*

Celebrations, family, cookouts, and fireworks are a common tradition. Enjoying those you love while having fun. What are some traditions you have or would like to start?

_____

_____

_____

_____

_____

_____

_____

_____

_____

_____

AUGUST

> *Affirmation: Today I do away with old habits and adopt new ones to help me move forward.*

After years of doing the same things over and over and not seeing change, today I announce my intent to change those unproductive things in my life. What are some habits you are willing to change?

_____
_____
_____
_____
_____
_____
_____
_____

SEPTEMBER

Affirmation: I am willing to focus on the good things in life that make me happy as I am transitioning that help me make better decisions leading to preferred results.

The season is changing, the air becomes crisp, and the colors of the world become golden. What are some things you like to do to welcome the fall season?

_____
_____
_____
_____
_____
_____
_____
_____
_____

OCTOBER

Affirmation: I absorb wisdom and knowledge easily as I broaden my horizons each day.

Cold nights, pumpkin carvings, and hot cider are ideal for October. It's a great time to curl up to a good book and wear cozy socks that warms the soul. What do you like to read on a cozy day?

_____
_____
_____
_____
_____
_____
_____
_____
_____

NOVEMBER

Affirmation: I am thankful for each new day filled with new mercies and endless possibilities.

Give thanks for your many blessings and reflect on all the things you are grateful for. Name some things you are thankful for and how you can express your gratitude towards them.

_____

_____

_____

_____

_____

_____

_____

_____

DECEMBER

Affirmation: I believe I am the creator of my life experiences.

Christmas is a time of giving to those you love and a time of giving to those less fortunate. It's also a great time for creating lasting memories with family and creating traditions that will last a lifetime. You reflect over your year and weigh your good/bad times. If you could go back and repeat your year, what are some things you would do differently?

Personal Goals For 20___

1._____

2._____

3._____

4._____

5._____

6._____

7._____

8._____

9._____

10._____

NOTE TO SELF
(Begin with I am…)

_____
_____
_____
_____
_____
_____
_____
_____
_____
_____
_____
_____
_____
_____
_____

RECOMMENDED READING

Reid, Twylia. *Broken Wings*. Savannah, Georgia: The Author's Pen, 2016.

About the Author

Twylia G. Reid is a native of Mississippi who currently resides in Savannah, Georgia, with her husband Dexter and son Mylon, a severe traumatic brain injury survivor. They are a blended Christian family of 4 adult children and 5 grandchildren. She obtained a B.S. Degree in Business Administration at Trident University International and is a 20-year US Army retiree.

Amazon #1 National/International Best Selling Author, 2019 Unspoken Wounds Woman Veteran's Portrait of Personal Courage Award Recipient, 2019 ACHI Magazine Woman of Achievement & Author of the Year Award Nominee, 2018 Congressional Black Caucus Featured Author, 2018 Winner of The Authors Show Female Non-Fiction Author, 2017 American Book Fest Best Book Awards Finalist, The Huffington Post Expert Feature Series "Who's Who –10 Black Female Experts to Watch in 2018" selectee, 2017 Indie Author Legacy Award Author of the Year finalist, President/CEO of *Broken Wings, Inc.*, speaker, group facilitator, and minister. She is also the founder of **Broken Wings Brain Injury Empowerment Group**, an online brain injury support group, and the Executive Producer/ Host of the ***Conquerors Café*** Podcast on Blog Talk Radio.

Passionate about her role as a brain injury advocate and caregiver, she was inspired to write her first book, **Broken Wings**, to encourage and inspire others affected by the devastation that brain injury causes.

About the Co-Author

NaSharee Davenport is a native of Mississippi who currently resides in Birmingham, AL, with her husband Robert and three children Tierra, Leah, and Dezmond.

She is an admin and group facilitator for Broken Wings Brain Injury Empowerment Group, an online support group which consists of brain injury survivors and caregivers. She's a co-author, a Pre-K teacher, Certified Tutor for Varsity Tutoring, and member of Zeta Phi Beta Sorority. She majored in Neuroscience Psychology at Birmingham Southern College where she received her inspiration for this field of study from her younger brother, Mylon, after he sustained a severe traumatic brain injury from a terrible car accident.

In her spare time, she loves to read and cook. NaSharee's love for others and her faith in God are paramount to her life and journey. She's a true testimony of resilience and triumph, and how affirmations can allow you to see yourself the way God sees you!

Additional books by Author Twylia G. Reid

"What Do You Do...When CAREGIVERS Need Care GIVEN" Caring for Yourself While Caring for Others

"When Caregivers Need Care Given Journal" Personal Journaling to Reflect on Your Emotions as a Caregiver One Day at a Time

"Affirmations for the Mind, Body & Soul" A Guide for Survivors of Traumatic Events

"A Survivor's Goal Planning Journal A Brain Injury Survivor's Guide to Goal Setting

"The WORD the Truth & The Light" BIBLE Study Notebook.

"Pray Receive Believe" Pray Journal

"SOARING By The Power Of God" 31 Day Devotional

"GET IT DONE" To Do List Planner

"But First...COFFEE" Monthly Planner

WE WANT TO HEAR FROM YOU

If this book has made a difference in your life I would be delighted to hear about it!

Leave a review on Amazon.com

BOOK TWYLIA TO SPEAK AT YOUR NEXT EVENT

Send an email to: **info@twyliareid.com**

Learn more about Twylia and her journey of hope and healing at:

www.TwyliaReid.com

If you would like to donate to help spread awareness about traumatic brain injury and the devastation it causes families please visit:

www.brokenwingsinc.org

FOLLOW TWYLIA ON SOCIAL MEDIA

Facebook Pages:
www.facebook.com/authortwyliareid
www.facebook.com/BWINC

Linked In: www.linkedin.com/in/twyliareid
Twitter: www.twitter.com/tgreid02
Instagram: www.instagram.com/twyliareid02

www.ingramcontent.com/pod-product-compliance
Lightning Source LLC
Chambersburg PA
CBHW051945160426
43198CB00013B/2302